Guidance notes and flow charts for the

Framework Contract

This contract should be used for the appointment of one or more suppliers to carry out construction work or to provide design or advisory services on an 'as instructed' basis over a set term

An NEC document

April 2013

Construction Clients' Board endorsement of NEC3

The Construction Clients' Board recommends that public sector organisations use the NEC3 contracts when procuring construction. Standardising use of this comprehensive suite of contracts should help to deliver efficiencies across the public sector and promote behaviours in line with the principles of *Achieving Excellence in Construction*.

Cabinet Office UK

NEC is a division of Thomas Telford Ltd, which is a wholly owned subsidiary of the Institution of Civil Engineers (ICE), the owner and developer of the NEC.

The NEC is a family of standard contracts, each of which has these characteristics:

- Its use stimulates good management of the relationship between the two parties to the contract and, hence, of the work included in the contract.
- It can be used in a wide variety of commercial situations, for a wide variety of types of work and in any location.
- It is a clear and simple document – using language and a structure which are straightforward and easily understood.

NEC3 Framework Contract is one of the NEC family. This document comprises the Framework Contract Guidance Notes and Flow Charts.

ISBN (complete box set) 978 0 7277 5867 5
ISBN (this document) 978 0 7277 5939 9
ISBN (Framework Contract) 978 0 7277 5901 6

First edition June 2005
Reprinted 2007, 2008, 2010
Reprinted with amendments 2013
Reprinted 2015, 2016, 2017, 2019, 2021, 2024

British Library Cataloguing in Publication Data for this publication is available from the British Library.

Typeset by Academic + Technical, Bristol

Printed and bound in Great Britain by Bell & Bain Limited, Glasgow, UK

CONTENTS

FOREWORD

I was delighted to be asked to write the Foreword for the NEC3 Contracts.

I have followed the outstanding rise and success of NEC contracts for a number of years now, in particular during my tenure as the 146th President of the Institution of Civil Engineers, 2010/11.

In my position as UK Government's Chief Construction Adviser, I am working with Government and industry to ensure Britain's construction sector is equipped with the knowledge, skills and best practice it needs in its transition to a low carbon economy. I am promoting innovation in the sector, including in particular the use of Building Information Modelling (BIM) in public sector construction procurement; and the synergy and fit with the collaborative nature of NEC contracts is obvious. The Government's construction strategy is a very significant investment and NEC contracts will play an important role in setting high standards of contract preparation, management and the desirable behaviour of our industry.

In the UK, we are faced with having to deliver a 15–20 per cent reduction in the cost to the public sector of construction during the lifetime of this Parliament. Shifting mind-set, attitude and behaviour into best practice NEC processes will go a considerable way to achieving this.

Of course, NEC contracts are used successfully around the world in both public and private sector projects; this trend seems set to continue at an increasing pace. NEC contracts are, according to my good friend and NEC's creator Dr Martin Barnes CBE, about better management of projects. This is quite achievable and I encourage you to understand NEC contracts to the best you can and exploit the potential this offers us all.

Peter Hansford

UK Government's Chief Construction Adviser
Cabinet Office

PREFACE

The NEC contracts are the only suite of standard contracts designed to facilitate and encourage good management of the projects on which they are used. The experience of using NEC contracts around the world is that they really make a difference. Previously, standard contracts were written mainly as legal documents best left in the desk drawer until costly and delaying problems had occurred and there were lengthy arguments about who was to blame.

The language of NEC contracts is clear and simple, and the procedures set out are all designed to stimulate good management. Foresighted collaboration between all the contributors to the project is the aim. The contracts set out how the interfaces between all the organisations involved will be managed – from the client through the designers and main contractors to all the many subcontractors and suppliers.

Versions of the NEC contract are specific to the work of professional service providers such as project managers and designers, to main contractors, to subcontractors and to suppliers. The wide range of situations covered by the contracts means that they do not need to be altered to suit any particular situation.

The NEC contracts are the first to deal specifically and effectively with management of the inevitable risks and uncertainties which are encountered to some extent on all projects. Management of the expected is easy, effective management of the unexpected draws fully on the collaborative approach inherent in the NEC contracts.

Most people working on projects using the NEC contracts for the first time are hugely impressed by the difference between the confrontational characteristics of traditional contracts and the teamwork engendered by the NEC. The NEC does not include specific provisions for dispute avoidance. They are not necessary. Collaborative management itself is designed to avoid disputes and it really works.

It is common for the final account for the work on a project to be settled at the time when the work is finished. The traditional long period of expensive professional work after completion to settle final payments just is not needed.

The NEC contracts are truly a massive change for the better for the industries in which they are used.

Dr Martin Barnes CBE

Originator of the NEC contracts

ACKNOWLEDGEMENTS

The first edition of the NEC Framework Contract was drafted by Peter Higgins working on behalf of the Institution of Civil Engineers, with the assistance of Les Eames and Dr Martin Barnes.

The original NEC was designed and drafted by Dr Martin Barnes then of Coopers and Lybrand, with the assistance of Professor J. G. Perry then of The University of Birmingham, T. W. Weddell, then of Travers Morgan Management, T. H. Nicholson, Consultant to the Institution of Civil Engineers, A. Norman, then of the University of Manchester Institute of Science and Technology, and P. A. Baird, then Corporate Contracts Consultant, Eskom, South Africa.

The Flow Charts were produced by Robert Gerrard with assistance from Ross Hayes and Tom Nicholson.

The members of the NEC Panel are:

P. Higgins, BSc, CEng, FICE, FCIArb (Chairman)
P. A. Baird, BSc, CEng, FICE, M(SA)ICE, MAPM
M. Barnes, BSc(Eng), PhD, FREng, FICE, FCIOB, CCMI, ACIArb, MBCS, FInstCES, FAPM
A. J. Bates, FRICS, MInstCES
A. J. M. Blackler, BA, LLB(Cantab), MCIArb
P. T. Cousins, BEng(Tech), DipArb, CEng, MICE, MCIArb, MCMI
L. T. Eames, BSc, FRICS, FCIOB
F. Forward, BA(Hons), DipArch, MSc(Const Law), RIBA, FCIArb
Professor J. G. Perry, MEng, PhD, CEng, FICE, MAPM
N. C. Shaw, FCIPS, CEng, MIMechE
T. W. Weddell, BSc, CEng, DIC, FICE, FIStructE, ACIArb

NEC Consultant:

R. A. Gerrard, BSc(Hons), MRICS, FCIArb, FCInstCES

Secretariat:

A. Cole, LLB, LLM, BL
J. M. Hawkins, BA(Hons), MSc
F. N. Vernon (Technical Adviser), BSc, CEng, MICE

AMENDMENTS

Full details of all amendments are available on www.neccontract.com.

GENERAL

The Framework Contract is designed to allow the *Employer* to invite tenders from suppliers to carry out work of on an 'as instructed' basis over a set term. Normally, the *Employer* will appoint a number of framework suppliers to carry out work within the defined scope.

Preparing the contract documents

When the *Employer* identifies the need for a framework arrangement, he will need to define the *scope* and the *end date*. The *scope* identifies the extent of work that is covered by the contract. It might refer to a specific location, identify the type of work to be carried out or other relevant information. The *scope* should be sufficiently defined that the *Employer* and *Supplier* are satisfied that the *Supplier* has the resources and capability to carry out the work likely to be instructed.

Work under a Package Order can be carried out under the conditions of any of the NEC Contracts. The NEC Professional Services Contract could be used for design and advisory services, and the NEC Engineering and Construction Contract or the NEC Engineering and Construction Short Contract for works. The *Employer* will select the most appropriate form for work under the framework, depending on the type and complexity of the work to be carried out.

The *Employer* prepares documents for inviting tenders for the Framework Contract. These are set out in the Contract Data for the Framework Contract and will include the following.

- The Framework Information, which contains information about the management of the Framework Contract. It will include the need for coordination meetings and other commitments which are not paid under a Time Charge Order or a Package Order.
- The Contract Data applicable to all time charge work – the appropriate entries from the Contract Data for the NEC Professional Services Contract conditions.
- The Contract Data applicable to all work under a Package Order – the appropriate entries from Contract Data for the selected contract conditions.
- The *selection procedure* – how the *Supplier* for a Work Package is to be selected. This may include providing a quotation for the work to be used in the selection.
- The *quotation procedure* – how the *Supplier* and *Employer* are to prepare and assess a quotation for a proposed Work Package.

The *Employer* must also describe the information required from tenderers for preparing a quotation – the *quotation information* – and other material needed to assess tenders or manage the Framework Contract.

Tenders are submitted, assessed by the *Employer* and a number of suppliers are selected and appointed under the Framework Contract.

Work under the Framework Contract

When the *Employer* has identified the need for some work within the *scope* of the Framework Contract, he provides the necessary additional Contract Data and selects the *Supplier* for the work using the *selection procedure*. This procedure sets out how a supplier is to be selected for a Time Charge Order and for a Package Order, and identifies at what stage a quotation is to be provided.

If advice is needed before the work for a Package Order can be fully defined, the selected *Supplier* can be instructed to help using a Time Charge Order. Once the work is fully defined, a supplier is selected for the proposed Work Package.

When a Time Charge Order is issued, the *Employer* must include the further Contract Data needed to define the work to be carried out – additional material in the Scope under the NEC Professional Services Contract. In addition, other entries from the NEC Professional Services Contract Contract Data, such as *starting date* and *completion date* must be given where relevant.

The work under a Time Charge Order is carried out under the NEC Professional Services Contract conditions, using the Options identified in the Contract Data of the Framework Contract, supplemented by the additional Contract Data provided by the *Employer*.

When the work is sufficiently defined, the *Employer* follows the *selection procedure* to identify the *Supplier* who will carry out the proposed Work Package. This procedure may include obtaining quotations for the work and using the quotations as part of the selection process. Alternatively, where it is possible to select a *Supplier* using other criteria, a quotation will be obtained from the chosen *Supplier* using the *quotation procedure*.

In either case, the quotation has to be prepared using the *quotation information* provided at tender, which will provide the source of the data to be used in the quotation. The quotation must comply with the *quotation procedure* set out by the *Employer*. This will set out the basis for preparing the quotation, and explain the amount of detail needed by the *Employer* to allow him to assess it.

As for time charge work, the *Employer* must provide the additional Contract Data for the proposed Work Package when he seeks a quotation.

The *Employer* can, when he receives the quotation, take a number of actions depending on his objectives. If he has received an acceptable quotation, he accepts it by issuing a Package Order to the appropriate *Supplier*. If he has not received an acceptable quotation, he may change the Work Package and ask for a revised quotation, or he may decide that the cost of the work is such that the Work Package should not be carried out.

The work under a Package Order is carried out under the NEC conditions of contract identified in the Contract Data of the Framework Contract, supplemented by the additional Contract Data provided by the *Employer*.

Further work can be instructed until the *end date*, unless termination takes place at an earlier date. Either Party is entitled to terminate at will. This means that no further work will be ordered under the framework contract, but any work already ordered, under either a Time Charge Order or a Package Order, continues, and can only be terminated under the contract conditions governing that work.

After the *end date*, unless otherwise agreed, no further work can be ordered. Work already instructed, under either a Time Charge Order or a Package Order, continues until it has been completed.

NEC3 contracts

The current list of published NEC3 contracts is stated below:

- NEC3 Engineering and Construction Contract (ECC)
- NEC3 Engineering and Construction Subcontract (ECS)
- NEC3 Engineering and Construction Short Contract (ECSC)
- NEC3 Engineering and Construction Short Subcontract (ECSS)
- NEC3 Professional Services Contract (PSC)
- NEC3 Professional Services Short Contract (PSSC)
- NEC3 Term Service Contract (TSC)
- NEC3 Term Service Short Contract (TSSC)
- NEC3 Supply Contract (SC)
- NEC3 Supply Short Contract (SSC)
- NEC3 Framework Contract (FC)
- NEC3 Adjudicator's Contract (AC)

For general guidance on when to use each contract refer to the NEC3 Procurement and Contract Strategies guide, available on www.neccontract.com.

Flow charts for the

Framework Contract

FLOW CHARTS

PREFACE

These flow charts depict the procedures followed when using the NEC3 Framework Contract (FC). They are intended to help people using the FC to see how the various FC clauses produce clear and precise sequences of action for the people involved.

The flow charts are not part of any contract. Much of the text and many of the words taken from the FC itself are abbreviated in the flow charts. The flow charts depict almost all of the sequences of action set out in the FC. Many of the sequences interact, and because of this, users of the flow charts will often have to review more than one sheet in order to track the full sequence of actions in one area.

ABBREVIATIONS USED IN THE FLOW CHART BOXES

FC 20	Flow chart for clause 20
E	*Employer*
S	*Supplier*
CD	Contract Data

Legend

CHART START

HEADINGS
    Headings in caps
    provide guidance

STATEMENTS
    If a clause is
    referenced, text
    is from the NEC

LOGIC LINKS
    Links go to right
    and/or downward
    unless shown

QUESTION
    Answer question
    to determine the
    route to follow

SUBROUTINE
    Include another
    flow chart here

CONTINUATION
    Link to matching
    point(s) on other
    chart sheets

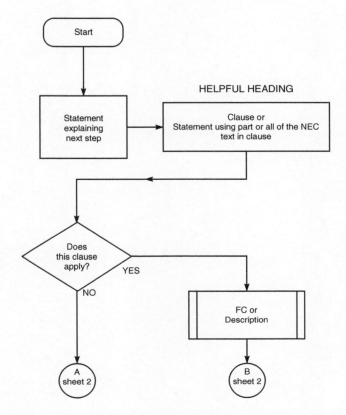

CHART TITLE
    Chart number,
    title and sheet

Flow chart or Sheet 1 of 2
Description

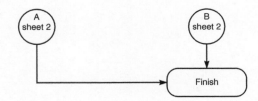

CONTINUATION

CHART FINISH

CHART TITLE

Flow chart or Sheet 2 of 2
Description

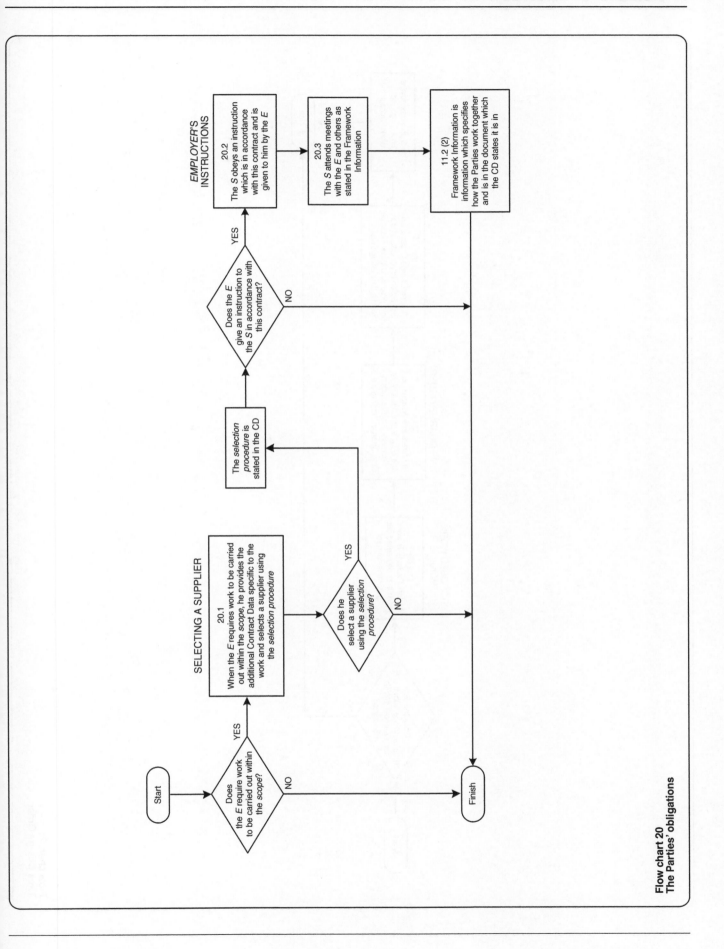

Flow chart 20
The Parties' obligations

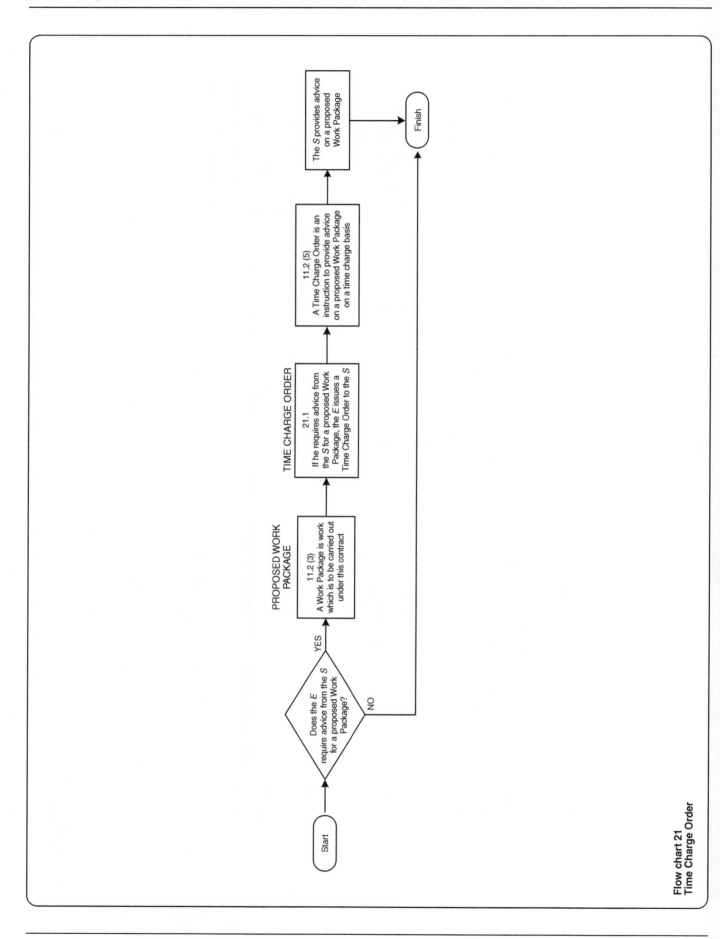

Flow chart 21
Time Charge Order

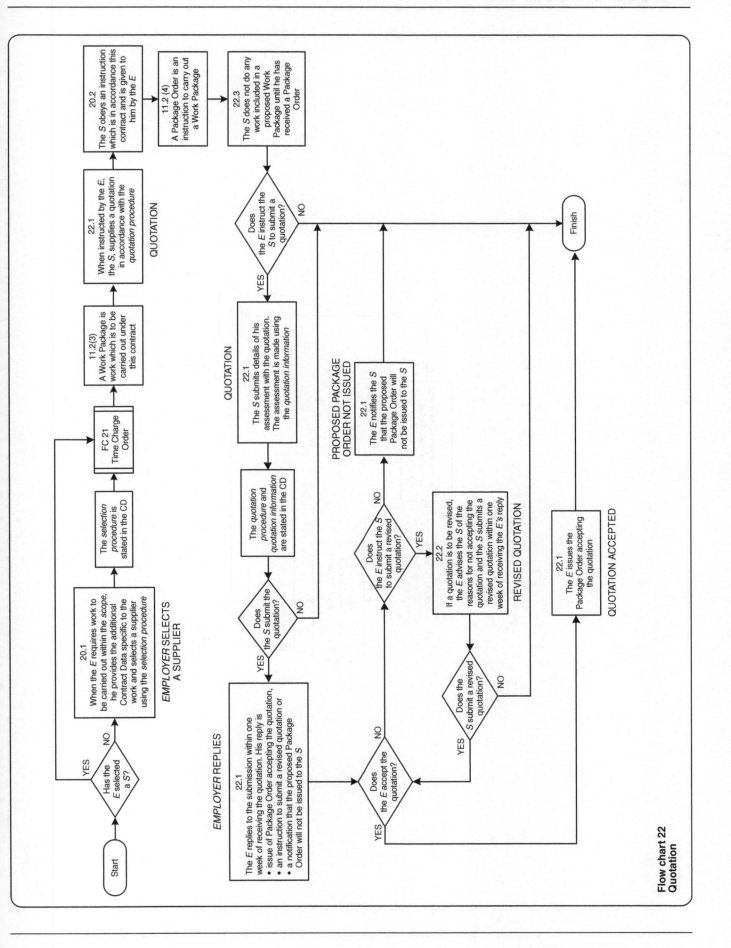

20.1
When the *E* requires work to be carried out within the *scope*, he provides the additional Contract Data specific to the work and selects a supplier using the *selection procedure*

EMPLOYER SELECTS A SUPPLIER

The *selection procedure* is stated in the CD

11.2(3)
A Work Package is work which is to be carried out under this contract

FC 21
Time Charge Order

22.1
When instructed by the *E*, the *S*, supplies a quotation in accordance with the *quotation procedure*

QUOTATION

20.2
The *S* obeys an instruction which is in accordance with the contract and is given to him by the *E*

11.2 (4)
A Package Order is an instruction to carry out a Work Package

22.3
The *S* does not do any work included in a proposed Work Package until he has received a Package Order

Has the *E* selected a *S*? — YES / NO

Start

QUOTATION

22.1
The *S* submits details of his assessment with the quotation. The assessment is made using the *quotation information*

The *quotation procedure* and *quotation information* are stated in the CD

Does the *S* submit the quotation? — YES / NO

Does the *E* instruct the *S* to submit a quotation? — YES / NO

EMPLOYER REPLIES

22.1
The *E* replies to the submission within one week of receiving the quotation. His reply is
• issue of Package Order accepting the quotation,
• an instruction to submit a revised quotation or
• a notification that the proposed Package Order will not be issued to the *S*

Does the *E* accept the quotation? — YES / NO

Does the *E* instruct the *S* to submit a revised quotation? — NO / YES

PROPOSED PACKAGE ORDER NOT ISSUED

22.1
The *E* notifies the *S* that the proposed Package Order will not be issued to the *S*

22.2
If a quotation is to be revised, the *E* advises the *S* of the reasons for not accepting the quotation and the *S* submits a revised quotation within one week of receiving the *E's* reply

REVISED QUOTATION

Does the *S* submit a revised quotation? — YES / NO

22.1
The *E* issues the Package Order accepting the quotation

QUOTATION ACCEPTED

Finish

Flow chart 22
Quotation

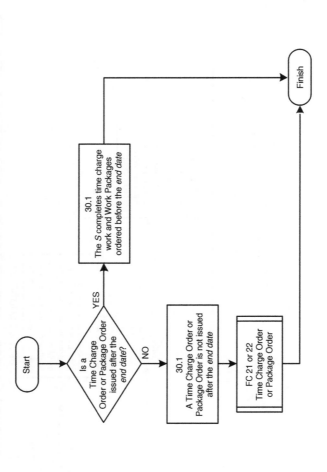

Start

Is a Time Charge Order or Package Order issued after the *end date*?

YES

30.1
The *S* completes time charge work and Work Packages ordered before the *end date*

NO

30.1
A Time Charge Order or Package Order is not issued after the *end date*

FC 21 or 22
Time Charge Order or Package Order

Finish

**Flow chart 30
Completion**

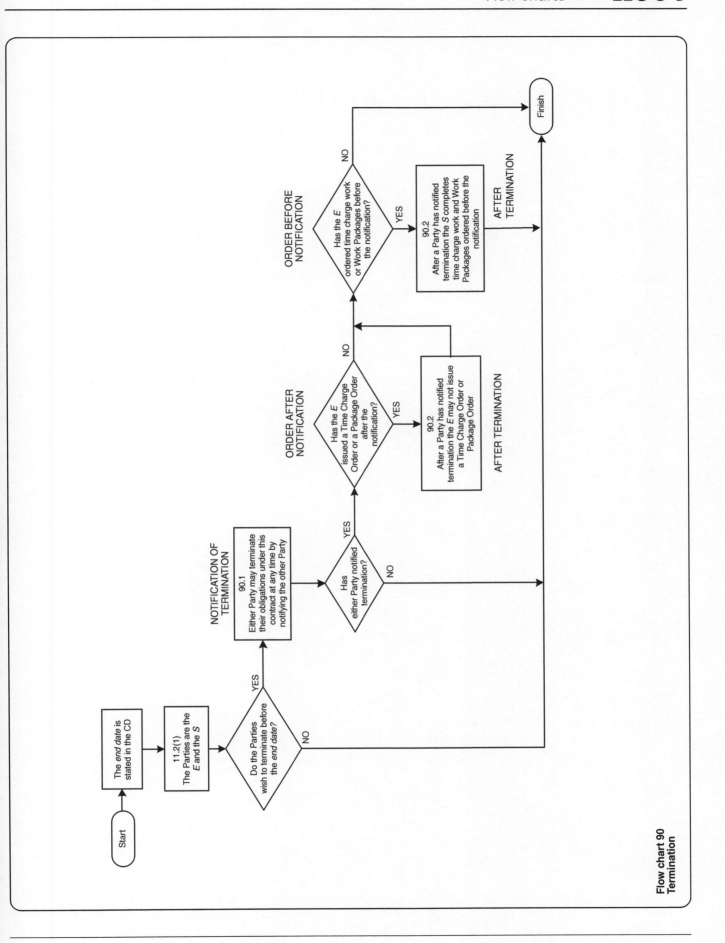

Flow chart 90
Termination

APPENDIX 1

Contract Data – worked example

Part one – Data provided by the *Employer*

The Data which will apply to all work under the Framework Contract is

- The conditions of this contract are **the clauses of the NEC3 Framework Contract April 2013.**
- The *Employer* is

  Name   **European Grain plc**
  Address   **Long Acre Industrial Estate**
             Spearshead
             Bristol
             BS8 2LR.

- The Framework Information is in **Part 1 of the enquiry document.**
- The *scope* is in **Part 2 of the enquiry document.**
- The *selection procedure* is in **Part 3 of the enquiry document.**
- The *quotation procedure* is in **Part 4 of the enquiry document.**
- The *end date* is **31 December 2016.**

The Data which will apply to all Time Charge Orders is

1 General

- The *conditions of contract* are the core clauses and the clauses for main Option **E**, dispute resolution Option **W2** and secondary Options **X1, X2 and X10** of the NEC3 Professional Services Contract April 2013.
- The *Employer* is

  Name   **European Grain plc**
  Address   **Long Acre Industrial Estate**
             Spearshead
             Bristol
             BS8 2LR.

- The *Adjudicator* is

  Name   **Ms I Arkwright**
  Address   **Meadow House**
             Goode Road
             Exeter
             EX8 6LM.

- The *services* are **project management of extensions to unloading and distribution facilities at Long Acre Works.**
- The *language of this contract* is **English.**
- The *law of the contract* is **the law of England and Wales, subject to the jurisdiction of the courts of England and Wales.**
- The *period for reply* is **2** weeks.
- The *period for retention* is **2** years following Completion or earlier termination.
- The *Adjudicator nominating body* is **The Construction Industry Council.**
- The *tribunal* is **arbitration.**

2 The Parties' main responsibilities

- The *Employer*'s *Agent* is

Name	**Mr F Giles**
Address	**Long Acre Industrial Estate**
	Spearshead
	Bristol
	BS8 2LR.

- The authority of the *Employer*'s *Agent* is **all actions by the *Employer* stated in this contract.**

5 Payment

- The *assessment interval* is **a calendar month.**
- The *currency of this contract* is **pounds sterling (£).**
- The *interest rate* is **2%** per annum above the **base lending rate of Lloyds Bank plc.**
- The expenses stated by the *Employer* are

item	amount
car mileage	35p per mile
rail travel	standard class fare.

- The *Consultant* prepares forecasts of the total Time Charge and *expenses* at intervals no longer than **4** weeks.
- The *index* is the **Retail Price Index.**

8 Indemnity, insurance and liability

- The amounts of insurance and the periods for which the *Consultant* maintains insurance are

event	cover	period following Completion of the whole of the *services* or earlier termination
failure of the *Consultant* to use the skill and care normally used by professionals providing services similar to the *services*	£5m in respect of each claim, without limit to the number of claims	6 years
death of or bodily injury to a person (not an employee of the *Consultant*) or loss of or damage to property resulting from an action or failure to take action by the *Consultant*	£5m in respect of each claim, without limit to the number of claims	12 months
death of or bodily injury to employees of the *Consultant* arising out of and in the course of their employment in connection with this contract	£2m in respect of each claim, without limit to the number of claims	12 months

Option W2

- The *arbitration procedure* is **The ICE Arbitration Procedure 1997.**
- The place where arbitration is to be held is **London.**
- The person or organisation who will choose an arbitrator
  - if the Parties cannot agree a choice or
  - if the *arbitration procedure* does not state who selects an arbitrator is **The Institution of Civil Engineers.**

The Data which will apply to all Package Orders is

1 General

- The *conditions of contract* are the core clauses and the clauses for main Option **C**, dispute resolution Option **W2** and secondary Options **X2 and Y(UK)2** of the NEC Engineering and Construction Contract April 2013.
- The *Employer* is

  Name   **European Grain plc**
  Address   **Long Acre Industrial Estate**
              Spearshead
              Bristol
              BS8 2LR.

- The *Project Manager* is

Name	**Mr F Giles**
Address	**Long Acre Industrial Estate**
	Spearshead
	Bristol
	BS8 2LR.

- The *Supervisor* is

Name	**Mr I Lookhard**
Address	**Long Acre Industrial Estate**
	Spearshead
	Bristol
	BS8 2LR.

- The *Adjudicator* is

Name	**Ms I Arkwright**
Address	**Meadow House**
	Goode Road
	Exeter
	EX8 6LM.

- The Works Information for all Work Packages is in **Parts 2 and 4 of the enquiry document.**

- The Site Information is in **Part 3 of the enquiry document.**

- The *language of this contract* is **English.**

- The *law of the contract* is **the law of England and Wales, subject to the jurisdiction of the courts of England and Wales.**

- The *period for reply* is **2** weeks.

- The *Adjudicator nominating body* is **The Construction Industry Council.**

- The *tribunal* is **arbitration.**

- The *Contractor* prepares forecasts of Defined Cost for the works at intervals no longer than **4** weeks.

3 Time

- The *Contractor* submits revised programmes at intervals no longer than **4** weeks.

4 Testing and Defects

- The *defects date* is **26** weeks after Completion of the whole of the *works*.

5 Payment

- The *currency of this contract* is **pounds sterling (£).**

- The *assessment interval* is **a calendar month.**

- The *Contractor's share percentages* and the *share ranges* are

share range	Contractor's share percentage
less than 80%	**30%**
from 80% to 120%	**50%**
greater than 120%	**80%**

8 Risks and insurance

- The minimum limit of indemnity for insurance in respect of loss of or damage to property (except the *works*, Plant and Materials and Equipment) and liability for bodily injury to or death of a person (not an employee of the *Contractor*) caused by activity in connection with this contract for any one event is **£2,000,000.**

- The minimum limit of indemnity for insurance in respect of death of or bodily injury to employees of the *Contractor* arising out of and in the course of their employment in connection with this contract for any one event is **unlimited.**

Option W2

- The *arbitration procedure* is **The ICE Arbitration Procedure 1997.**
- The place where arbitration is to be held is **London.**
- The person or organisation who will choose an arbitrator
  - if the Parties cannot agree a choice or
  - if the *arbitration procedure* does not state who selects an arbitrator is **The Institution of Civil Engineers.**

Part two – Data provided by the *Supplier*

The Data which will apply to all work under the Framework Contract is

- The *Supplier* is

Name	**PM Services Ltd**
Address	**27 Enterprise Way**
	Bristol
	BS9 6PM.

- The *quotation information* is in **Schedule 1.**

The Data which will apply to all Time Charge Orders is

- The *Consultant* is

Name	**PM Services Ltd**
Address	**27 Enterprise Way**
	Bristol
	BS9 6PM.

- The *key people* are

Name	**Mr. M. Jones**
Job	**Project Manager**
Responsibilities	**In charge of the project**
Qualifications	**MSc, MIMechE**
Experience	**3 years as Project Manager, 4 years as Assistant PM.**

- The *staff rates* are detailed in **Schedule 2.**

- The *expenses* stated by the *Consultant* are

item	amount
Subsistence	**£80 per night.**
(as authorised	
away from home	
address)	

The Data which will apply to all Package Orders is

- The *Contractor* is

Name	**PM Services Ltd**
Address	**27 Enterprise Way**
	Bristol
	BS9 6PM.

- The *direct fee percentage* is **9%.**

- The *subcontracted fee percentage* is **7%.**

- The key people are detailed in **Schedule 3.**